# Who?

Mary Elizabeth Salzmann

Published by SandCastle™, an imprint of ABDO Publishing Company, 4940 Viking Drive, Edina, Minnesota 55435.

Printed in the United States.

Photo credits: Adobe, Comstock, CORBIS/Richard Fukuhara, Corel, PhotoDisc

Library of Congress Cataloging-in-Publication Data

Salzmann, Mary Elizabeth, 1968-
      Who? / Mary Elizabeth Salzmann.
         p. cm. -- (Do you wonder?)
      Summary: Simple questions and answers about people, using the word "who."
      ISBN 1-57765-169-3 (alk. paper) -- ISBN 1-57765-281-9 (set)
         1. Readers (Primary) 2. Readers--Children's questions and answers. [1. Readers.
      2. Questions and answers.] I. Title.

      PE1119 .S235 2000
      428.1--dc21

                                                                        99-046489

The SandCastle concept, content, and reading method have been reviewed and approved by a national advisory board including literacy specialists, librarians, elementary school teachers, early childhood education professionals, and parents.

## Let Us Know

After reading the book, SandCastle would like you to tell us your stories about reading. What is your favorite page? Was there something hard that you needed help with? Share the ups and downs of learning to read. We want to hear from you! To get posted on the Abdo Publishing Company Web site, send us email at:

**sandcastle@abdopub.com**

# About SandCastle™

A professional team of educators, reading specialists, and content developers created the SandCastle™ series to support young readers as they develop reading skills and strategies and increase their general knowledge. The SandCastle™ series has four levels that correspond to early literacy development in young children. The levels are provided to help teachers and parents select the appropriate books for young readers.

**Emerging Readers**
(no flags)

**Beginning Readers**
(1 flag)

**Transitional Readers**
(2 flags)

**Fluent Readers**
(3 flags)

These levels are meant only as a guide. All levels are subject to change.

To see a complete list of SandCastle™ books and other nonfiction titles from ABDO Publishing Company, visit **www.abdopub.com** or contact us at:
4940 Viking Drive, Edina, Minnesota 55435 • 1-800-800-1312 • fax: 1-952-831-1632

I use the word **who** to ask questions about persons.

**Who** feeds our dog breakfast?

My little brother and I feed our dog breakfast.

**Who** shows me where to find books?

The librarian shows me where to find books.

**Who** feeds the birds
with me?

My sister feeds the birds
with me.

**Who** wades in the stream with me?

My friend wades in the stream with me.

**Who** plays golf with me?

Grandpa plays golf
with me.

**Who** carries me on his shoulders?

Dad carries me on his shoulders.

**Who** helps me ride my bike?

Mom helps me ride my bike.

**Who** reads with me at bedtime?

Grandma reads with me at bedtime.

# Words I Can Read

## Nouns

A noun is a person, place, or thing

bedtime (BED-time) p. 21
bike (BIKE) p. 19
breakfast (BREK-fuhst) p. 7
brother (BRUHTH-ur) p. 7
Dad (DAD) p. 17
dog (DOG) p. 7
friend (FREND) p. 13
golf (GOLF) p. 15

Grandma (GRAND-ma) p. 21
Grandpa (GRAND-pa) p. 15
librarian (lye-BRER-ee-uhn) p. 9
Mom (MOM) p. 19
sister (SISS-tur) p. 11
stream (STREEM) p. 13
word (WURD) p. 5

## Plural Nouns

A plural noun is more than one person, place, or thing

birds (BURDZ) p. 11
books (BUKSS) p. 9
persons (PUR-suhnz) p. 5

questions (KWESS-chuhnz) p. 5
shoulders (SHOHL-dur) p. 17

## Pronouns

A pronoun is a word that replaces a noun

I (EYE) pp. 5, 7
me (MEE) pp. 9, 11, 13, 15, 17, 19, 21

who (HOO) pp. 5, 7, 9, 11, 13, 15, 17, 19, 21

# Verbs

A verb is an action or being word

ask (ASK) p. 5

carries (KA-reez) p. 17

feed (FEED) p. 7

feeds (FEEDZ) pp. 7, 11

find (FINDE) p. 9

helps (HELPSS) p. 19

plays (PLAYZ) p. 15

reads (REEDZ) p. 21

ride (RIDE) p. 19

shows (SHOHZ) p. 9

use (YOOZ) p. 5

wades (WAYDZ) p. 13

# Adjectives

An adjective describes something

his (HIZ) p. 17

little (LIT-uhl) p. 7

my (MYE) pp. 7, 11, 13, 19

our (OUR) p. 7

# Adverbs

An adverb tells how, when, or where
something happens

where (WAIR) p. 9

23

# Glossary

**bedtime** – the time when you usually go to sleep.

**breakfast** – the first meal of the day.

**golf** – a game in which players use clubs to try and hit a small white ball into a series of holes.

**librarian** – a person who works in a library and helps people find books and information.

**shoulders** – the parts of your body between your arms and your neck.

**stream** – a brook or small river.